C000182523

On Cambrian Lines

Derek Huntriss

First published 1993

ISBN 0 7110 2185 6

© Derek Huntriss 1993

Published by

IAN ALLAN *Publishing*

Shepperton, Surrey; and printed by Ian Allan Printing Ltd at its
works at Coombelands in Runnymede, England.

Front Cover:
After climbing the two miles of 1 in 52 from Llanbrynmair station, BR Standard Class 4 4-6-0s Nos 75053
and 75063 attack the last mile of 1 in 56 to Talerddig
summit with the up 'Cambrian Coast Express' on
28 December 1965. *T. B. Owen*

Rear Cover:
The summit of Cader Idris (2,927ft above sea level) and
the nearer, more prominent, ridge of Craig Las form the
backdrop for this picture of Standard 4 4-6-0 No 75021
as it heads a south-bound passenger train across the
timber trestle section of Barmouth Bridge on 9 August
1963. *T. B. Owen*

This page:
'Manor' class 4-6-0 No 7828 *Odney Manor* leaves
Aberystwyth MPD for the station prior to departure
with the up 'Cambrian Coast Express' in August 1963.
D. Penney

Introduction

Originating from a collection of independent companies, the Cambrian Railways Co was formed on 25 July 1864 with its headquarters and works at Oswestry. Developing a route length of around 300 miles and being surrounded by the GWR, it nevertheless became the largest railway company to operate in Wales until being absorbed into the GWR in 1922.

Whereas other pre-Grouping companies managed to retain much of their former identity after 1923, the GWR was determined to make a clean sweep and banish all Cambrian Railways' memories. They carried out vast track layout alterations and improvements, the once familiar long-armed Cambrian signals giving way to the more modern lower quadrant type.

From then on every decade saw changes in motive power right up to the end of steam traction in March 1967. The early 1930s even saw the removal of the first GWR replacements, in particular the 2-4-0 'Stella' and 'Barham' classes. The smaller GWR 4-4-0s, the '3521' class, became extinct, and the mainstay of Cambrian motive power became 'Duke' class 4-4-0s and Standard 0-6-0 goods. By 1960, the last of the 'Dean Goods' 0-6-0s had been withdrawn and the 'Dukedog' 4-4-0s were in their final year of operation. The 1950s had seen the introduction of several types of BR Standard locos, including the 75xxx series 4-6-0s and 78xxx series 2-6-0s. Other newcomers were the 80xxx and 82xxx series tank locomotives, in addition to the Ivatt 465xx 2-6-0s. Surviving ex-GWR classes were the '2251' class 0-6-0 goods, '73xx' 2-6-0s and 'Manor' 4-6-0s.

It was this mix of well-kept motive power that took the Cambrian lines up to 1963 when they were handed over to the London Midland Region. From then on, surviving Western Region pride took a battering, and once-spotless 'Manors' were allowed to degenerate into scruffy, unkempt engines of no noticeable distinction.

For the first time in colour, this title portrays the former Cambrian Railways routes in the 1950s and 1960s as seen by the dedicated photographers whose work makes up the contents of this book. The title is set out in three basic sections: the first taking the reader on a journey from Aberystwyth to Borth; the second from Portmadoc to Shrewsbury; and the final section describes several other Cambrian routes, including the narrow gauge Vale of Rheidol and Welshpool & Llanfair railways.

Today, journeys on both of these narrow gauge railways can still be enjoyed and, with the introduction of BR's 'Cardigan Bay Express' on 25 May 1987, main line Cambrian steam is once again a reality.

Bibliography

G. F. Bannister: *Branch Line Byways – Vol 2 – Central Wales*; Atlantic Transport Publishers

Keith M. Beck: *The Great Western North of Wolverhampton*; Ian Allan

Rex Christiansen & R. W. Miller: *The Cambrian Railways Vols 1 & 2*; David & Charles

T. P. Dalton: *Cambrian Companionship*; Oxford Publishing Co

C. C. Green: *Cambrian Railways Album Vols 1 & 2*; Ian Allan

Peter Johnson: *Railway World Special: The Welsh Narrow Gauge Railways*; Ian Allan

Rex Kennedy: *Steam on the Cambrian*; Ian Allan

R. W. Kidner: *The Cambrian Railways*; The Oakwood Press

W. G. Rear & M. F. Williams: *Scenes from the Past No 4 – The Cambrian Coast Railway*; Foxline Publishing

Magazines: *Trains Illustrated*; *Modern Railways*; *Backtrack*; *Railway Magazine*; *Steam Railway*; *Steam World*; *Railway World*

Other Publications: *Cambrian Railways Timetable – 1902*; *Working Timetable GWR – 1939*; *Working Timetables BR (WR)* for 1954, 1957/58 and 1962/63; *Sectional Appendix to the Working Timetable – Shrewsbury District 1960*

Acknowledgements

Thanks are offered to all the dedicated photographers whose irreplaceable work appears in these pages, in particular to Trevor Owen, without whose co-operation this title could not have been contemplated.

Additional thanks are due to Geoffrey Bannister and his son Andrew who were prepared to spend a considerable time sharing their in-depth knowledge of the former Cambrian Railways system.

Derek Huntriss

Camborne
Cornwall
May 1993

Right:
Operating from the 1924 Vale of Rheidol station, No 7 *Owain Glyndŵr* prepares to leave with the 1.45pm service to Devil's Bridge on August Bank Holiday Monday – 1 August 1960. *M. Mensing*

Now preserved ex-GWR 4-6-0 No 7822 *Foxcote Manor* stands alongside BR Standard Class 4 4-6-0 No 75023 and Class 4 2-6-4T No 80099 outside Aberystwyth MPD in August 1963. After the take-over of the Cambrian Railways by the GWR, the old Cambrian locomotive shed was demolished and partly rebuilt in 1922; the present modern two-road depot was erected in 1938. Extensive track layout alterations and improvements accompanied the introduction of GWR lower quadrant semaphores.

Following the cessation of BR steam operation over the lines in March 1967, the MPD at Aberystwyth (a sub-shed to Machynlleth) was converted to house the motive power and some coaching stock from the Vale of Rheidol Railway. It carries out the same function under private ownership to this day. *D. Penney*

The 'larger' engines, ie 'Manors' and '43xx' 2-6-0s, did not arrive on the Cambrian until the early years of World War 2, when extra power was necessitated by increased traffic levels. From February 1941 'Moguls' began to appear on freight workings and, during the 1950s, the '43xx' 2-6-0s arrived in increasing numbers, first at Aberystwyth and later Machynlleth. Prior to World War 2, the Cambrian lines were classified as 'yellow' in the GWR's route allocation scheme, dictating that anything larger than a 'Duke' or 'Earl' 4-4-0 was not permitted.

Here, No 6342 awaits its next turn of duty at Aberystwyth MPD on 2 August 1959. *W. Potter*

Above:
Ex-GWR 'Manor' No 7802 *Bradley Manor* departs from Aberystwyth with the 'Cambrian Coast Express' on 31 October 1964. Alongside, sister locomotive, No 7803 *Barcote Manor*, awaits departure with the 10.20am Class B passenger train to Shrewsbury. This train would stop at all stations. The platform awnings, covering the entire platform width, are clearly visible. *T. B. Owen*

Right:
The crisp lighting conditions of 22 December 1958 see 'Manor' No 7801 *Anthony Manor* passing the motive power depot at Aberystwyth with a passenger train for Shrewsbury. Introduced in 1938, the lightweight 'Manor' class 4-6-0s were initially shunned by their crews in favour of the elderly 'Bulldog' 4-4-0s. Following transfer to the Newton Abbot division during the summer of 1948, the steaming problems of this class really came to light. Their shortcomings were once again highlighted at Swindon in 1951 after tests on the new BR Standard Class 4 4-6-0s. Following modifications to the chimney and blastpipe, and adjustments to the firebars in the grate, their reputation as a lame duck was transformed into that of a first-rate medium-power locomotive of the highest Swindon traditions. *T. B. Owen*

Ex-GWR Collett '2251' class 0-6-0 No 2260 attacks the 1 in 75 climb from Llanbadarn at Fron Fraith with an Aberystwyth-Shrewsbury passenger train on 16 May 1959. Following the downgrading of power classification of the 'Dukedog' 4-4-0s in the mid-1950s from 'B' category to 'A' in the 'Yellow' classification, five '2251' class 0-6-0s were allocated to Aberystwyth for freight and local passenger workings. The '2251' class had become associated with the Cambrian in 1937 and proved to be capable performers on a wide variety of duties, including goods and local passenger workings. They found favour with footplate crews who had much better protection from the elements than on the exposed footplates of the 'Dean Goods' 0-6-0s. *T. B. Owen*

Approaching Llanbadarn Crossing with a passenger train for Aberystwyth on 2 August 1958, the fireman of ex-GWR 'Dukedog' 4-4-0 No 9015 prepares to hand over the single-line token from Bow Street before entering the double-track section for the remainder of the journey into Aberystwyth.

Almost two years later, in May 1960, driver Tim Abrahams and fireman G. Hughes of Aberystwyth had the dubious pleasure of taking No 9015, the last of Aberystwyth's 'Dukedogs', on its final journey to Swindon and the graveyard. *T. B. Owen*

Left:
From about 1953 onwards, many of the older classes of
locomotive were removed from the stock-books and
replaced by the new BR Standard classes. Of six new
Standard Class 2 2-6-0 78xxx locomotives allocated to
Machynlleth, Nos 78002 and 78003 were stationed at
Portmadoc where they replaced some ex-Cambrian
0-6-0s. Received with mixed feelings, the tender cab of
the 2-6-0s provided much needed protection when
working tender-first, especially on the exposed coastal
section from Dovey Junction to Pwllheli.

Here, No 78007 works away from Llanbadarn Crossing, a notorious accident blackspot, with a passenger
working from Aberystwyth. *T. B. Owen*

Right:
Following removal of heavy lineside undergrowth,
'Manor' No 7823 *Hook Norton Manor* climbs Fron
Fraith bank towards Bow Street with the up 'Cambrian
Coast Express' on 25 April 1962. This was one of a
batch of 10 locomotives, Nos 7820-7829, which entered
service some three years after Nationalisation.
Although the batch was completed in November and
December 1950, an excess of mixed-traffic 4-6-0s on
the Western Region led to Nos 7828 *Odney Manor* and
7829 *Ramsbury Manor* being put into store for 14
months before delivery to their first depot, Neath (87A),
in February 1952. *T. B. Owen*

Left:
Allocated to Shrewsbury (89A) MPD, 'Standard' 4-6-0 No 75005 hauls a mixed rake of blood and custard liveried stock away from Bow Street towards Aberystwyth on 21 April 1954. The then new Standard Class 4s were not generally popular with local footplate crews, particularly when used on pick-up goods workings in and out of sidings, where they were considered to be clumsy and very prone to slipping. *T. B. Owen*

Above:
'Manor' No 7803 *Barcote Manor* heads a Birmingham-Aberystwyth train away from Bow Street on 16 May 1959. The flat-topped Cambrian distant for Bow Street can be seen on the right of the picture.

Whilst some members of the 'Manor' class had chequered careers with many moves, a few hardly moved at all. Along with No 7802 *Bradley Manor*, No 7803 spent the majority of its working life, until January 1965, at Aberystwyth. Regular performers on the 'Cambrian Coast Express', the two locomotives were always kept in superb condition by shed staff. *T. B. Owen*

Above:

The up 6pm mail from Aberystwyth to York is seen between Bow Street and Llandre behind BR Standard Class 4 No 75016 on 20 August 1966. Known locally as the 'Second Mail', the usual consist for this train was four mail vans and three passenger coaches. Here, No 75016 is attacking the one mile and 47 chains of

1 in 75 from Bow Street to Llandre. After Llandre there followed two miles and 43 chains at falling gradients of 1 in 75 and 1 in 60. *T. B. Owen*

Right:

Badly leaking steam, 'Standard' 4-6-0 No 75063 heads the up 'Cambrian Coast Express' away from the platforms at Bow Street on 28 December 1965. Allocated to Shrewsbury (6D) MPD in September 1964, No 75063 survived as a regular Cambrian line performer until withdrawn in June 1966. *T. B. Owen*

Drifting down the last few yards of 1 in 60 between Llandre and Borth, 'Dukedog' No 9015 heads an Aberystwyth-Machynlleth passenger train on 2 August 1958. Announced by the Great Western as new engines for its Cambrian section in 1936, it was widely believed that they would be Swindon thoroughbreds. The fact was that the 'Earl' class, as the type became later known, were mongrels.

The prototype 'Dukedog' No 3265 *Tre Pol And Pen* had appeared in 1930 at a time when there was no need for further rebuilds. However, six years later, the motive power situation had changed and was aggravated by increasing failures of the 'Duke' class as a result of mainframe weakening. The short-term solution lay in rebuilding 'Duke' class boilers on to the stronger 'Bulldog' frames, producing a hybrid loco that fell into

the permitted axle-loading for the Cambrian at that time.

In an effort to clear the 32xx number series for a new batch of Collett 0-6-0s in 1946, the 'Dukedogs', as they eventually came to be known, were renumbered into the 90xx series. Today, only one member of the 'Dukedog' class, No 9017, survives in preservation on the Bluebell Railway. *T. B. Owen*

'Standard' 4-6-0 No 75013 passes a former Cambrian distant as it works an unidentified Shrewsbury-Aberystwyth freight away from Borth on 18 March 1966. On this day of clear weather, the foothills of the Cambrian Mountains beyond Aberdovey are clearly visible. Reallocated from Machynlleth (6F) MPD to Shrewsbury (6D) MPD in December 1966, No 75013 saw service at Croes Newydd (6C) and Stoke (5D) MPDs before withdrawal in August 1967. After a period of three months in store at Stoke, it was despatched to Birds' scrapyard at Long Marston where it was cut up during February 1968. *T. B. Owen*

Above:
Displaying its 89C shedplate and carrying a separate top-feed boiler, a feature not found on every member of this class, 'Dukedog' 4-4-0 No 9021 stands outside the two-road sub-shed at Portmadoc in August 1958. Situated at the Pwllheli end of the up platform, the depot was in close proximity to housing which meant that footplate crews had to be careful about smoke emission and noise. This problem disappeared when the sub-shed closed in August 1963. *P. Hughes*

Right:
Against the backdrop of the quarry north of Minffordd, 'Manors' Nos 7819 *Hinton Manor* and 7822 *Foxcote Manor* head the return working of the Royal Train from Aberdovey on the occasion of the visit of HM The Queen and HRH The Duke of Edinburgh to the Outward Bound School on 9 August 1963. Today, both locomotives are still active in preservation. *T. B. Owen*

Left:
This timeless study depicts Collett 0-6-0 No 2232 shunting the yard at Minffordd on 29 March 1957. The tracks of the narrow-gauge Festiniog Railway are clearly visible. At that time, when shunting work was to be carried out in the yard, a pilot locomotive would be attached to a train from Portmadoc and detached at Minffordd. After using the train staff to open the frame for the yard, the pilot loco would be detached and proceed to the goods yard, the through train proceeding on its way. After performing its shunting duties, the loco would regain the main line later in the day, working forward to Penrhyndeudraeth ` where it would be detached before working back to Portmadoc. *J. M. Jarvis*

Above:
'Dukedog' 4-4-0s Nos 9017 and 9014 are pictured having arrived at Minffordd with a Festiniog Railway Society special in April 1958. *D. Penney*

Above:
On 9 August 1963, Ivatt '2MT' 2-6-0 No 46511 leaves Barmouth with a passenger train for Machynlleth. A fine example of a 1960s 'National' petrol tanker can be seen delivering its contents to a garage on the right of the picture. The most important intermediate station on the 54 miles from Pwllheli to Dovey Junction,

Barmouth was the terminus for most trains from the Dolgellau and Ruabon line, as well as some from Pwllheli working south, and Machynlleth working north. *T. B. Owen*

Right:
9 August 1963 was probably the most important day in

the life of Pwllheli MPD, when it was host to four of the six 'Manor' class engines involved with the Royal Train working. Here, 'Manors' Nos 7827 *Lydham Manor* and 7828 *Odney Manor* cross over the lifeboat slipway as they leave Barmouth Bridge *en route* to Pwllheli. *T. B. Owen*

Left:
BR Standard Class 2 2-6-2T No 82033 approaches Barmouth from the bridge with a passenger working from Machynlleth to Barmouth on 9 August 1963. The engineer responsible for the planning of the bridge, Henry Coneybeare, had to design a structure which allowed for the considerable amount of navigation which served the mines and quarries of the Mawddach Estuary hinterland, nearly eight miles inland, during the early 1860s. Initially, a channel for shipping on the

Barmouth side had to be accommodated by a movable section, initially a drawbridge, but later a swingbridge. This section was approached from the southern side by a fixed viaduct of wooden trestles, supported on 500 timber piles. There are 113 spans over water throughout. *T. B. Owen*

Above:
On a perfect summer evening, 'Dukedog' No 9004 arrives at Barmouth with a passenger train; Cader Idris

and the more prominent ridge of Craig Las are clearly visible in the background. In 1932, the setting of the bridge was used in the making of the first film version of 'The Ghost Train', a perennial stage and screen thriller written by Arnold Ridley of 'Dad's Army' fame. Models used in the superimposed crash sequence were supplied by the well known firm of W. J. Bassett-Lowke of Nottingham. *P. B. Whitehouse/Colour-Rail*

Above:
Standard Class 4 No 75002 clings to the cliff-side as it approaches the landslip shelter at Friog with an unidentified Pwllheli-Shrewsbury goods working on 5 August 1966. After a second serious accident at this location – on 4 March 1933 when the 6.10am morning mail struck fallen debris at this spot, sending the locomotive to the shore below and killing its crew – the

GWR took measures to make sure it would not happen again. Visible to the right of the oncoming train is a section of cliff-face that has been strengthened with masonry and, nearer to the camera, it has been strengthened with relieving arches. A final section of concrete avalanche shelter was constructed with a pitched roof to direct any falling debris on to the shore below.
W. Potter

Right:
Specially prepared at Oswestry, 'Manors' Nos 7819 *Hinton Manor* and 7822 *Foxcote Manor* leave Towyn with the ecs from the Royal Train on 10 August 1963.
D. Penney

Above:
'Manors' Nos 7827 *Lydham Manor* and 7828 *Odney Manor* stand at the head of the ecs Royal Train at Aberdovey in August 1963. Both locomotives were eventually to be preserved. *D. Penney*

Right:
'Standard' 2-6-2T No 82033 skirts the Dovey estuary after leaving Aberdovey with the Pwllheli portion of the 'Cambrian Coast Express' on 9 August 1963. Known as the 'deviation', this section of line gained this name because it replaced a scheme, planned to bridge the Dovey between Aberdovey and Ynyslas which was abandoned owing to high costs. One of 11 'Standard' 2-6-2Ts nominally allocated to Machynlleth at that time, No 82033 had arrived on Cambrian lines from Bristol Barrow Road (82E) MPD in December 1960. Following 12 months allocation to Bangor (6H) MPD commencing in April 1965, No 82033 continued her career on the Southern Region of BR until her withdrawal from traffic in September 1965. After two months in store at Nine Elms (70A) MPD, No 82033 joined three of her classmates at Birds' scrapyard at Risca where they were broken up. *T. B. Owen*

Having just crossed the timber trestle bridge over the River Dovey, an unidentified BR 'Standard' 4-6-0 enters Dovey Junction with the Pwllheli portion of the 'Cambrian Coast Express' on 18 March 1966. The Aberystwyth portion of this train has already arrived, the locomotive working this portion being out of picture to the right. At Dovey Junction the two portions were joined for the remainder of the journey to Shrewsbury and Paddington. Much of the layout, station buildings and signalbox at this time dated from rebuilding which took place in 1958. Despite its spectacular setting, this exposed location was, and still is, vulnerable to flooding, high tides often covering the tracks. *T. B. Owen*

Prior to attaching the Pwllheli portion of the 'Cambrian Coast Express', 'Manor' No 7802 *Bradley Manor* has arrived with the Aberystwyth portion on 27 December 1961. With only two platform faces, station working at Dovey Junction was complicated, particularly when it became necessary to combine and detach portions as well as crossing trains. The GWR/WR semaphores survived until the summer of 1988 when they were replaced as part of the junction layout remodelling. *T. B. Owen*

Above:
Unidentified members of the BR 'Standard' 4-6-0 and Ivatt 2-6-0 classes double-head a Shrewsbury-Pwllheli freight on 18 March 1966. In the consist are two gunpowder vans. These were presumably destined for Cookes Explosives Ltd at Penrhyndeudraeth, who had daily movements of the company's products. Much of the coast line traffic was stone quarried by the Pwllheli Granite Co, which was situated between Minffordd and Portmadoc. The remaining traffic was often coal, supplemented by agricultural produce and livestock. There was a limited amount of slate traffic, consisting of the occasional wagon load rather than regular consignments. *T. B. Owen*

Right:
This delightful study depicts a BR 'Standard' 4-6-0 heading the up 'Cambrian Coast Express' in the Dovey valley between Dovey Junction and Machynlleth on 19 March 1966. *T. B. Owen*

Left:
BR Standard Class 4 No 75002 approaches Machynlleth station with a Pwllheli-Paddington passenger train on 20 August 1966. Absorbed into the GWR empire in 1922, this part of the Cambrian was originally promoted by the Newtown & Machynlleth Railway. It was opened from Pwllheli in May 1862 for goods and in January 1863 for passenger traffic.

Earlier, in 1859, the 2ft 3in gauge Corris Railway had opened its line to Aberllefenny. The former exchange sidings with the Corris are just out of the picture to the right. The goods accommodation in the foreground was a late addition (in 1964), and was opened as a result of the closure of the route from Ruabon to Morfa Mawddach. *T. B. Owen*

Above:
Also on 20 August 1966, sister locomotive No 75047 departs from the east end of Machynlleth station with another Pwllheli-Paddington passenger working. By this time diesel traction in the form of DMUs had displaced steam on many Cambrian section passenger services. Here, No 75047 appears to have received the attentions of visiting enthusiasts prior to its working to Shrewsbury. *T. B. Owen*

Following several years' allocation to Wrexham (84K) MPD and two months' allocation to Shrewsbury (84G) MPD at the beginning of 1960, 'Standard' 2-6-2T No 82021 arrived at Machynlleth in March 1960. It carries the green livery applied to members of the class allocated to Western Region MPDs. To move the 'Standard' 2-6-2T it required two men to operate the turntable at Machynlleth, as seen in this picture taken in June 1963. Following the introduction of DMUs to some Cambrian line services, No 82021 was allocated to Nine Elms (70A) MPD in April 1965, only to be withdrawn six months later. *G. Rixon*

Pictured on the 'back road' at Machynlleth MPD on 27 August 1959, 'Dukedog' No 9018 awaits its next turn of duty. In 1947 only a handful of the newly-constructed 'Manor' class 4-6-0s had reached the Cambrian main line, leaving 20 'Dukedogs' and four 'Dukes' to handle the brunt of the work. Normal allocations were to Oswestry, Machynlleth and Aberystwyth, with one or two at the sub-sheds at Portmadoc and Pwllheli. During the summer months heavier trains required double-heading, a pair of these magnificent machines making a fine sight on the climb to Talerddig. By the end of 1955, seven of the 29 'Dukedogs' had been withdrawn and the survivors reduced to power Class 'A'. *W. Potter*

Left:
Following the Dovey valley between Machynlleth and Cemmes Road, BR 'Standard' 4-6-0 No 75012 heads the up 'Cambrian Coast Express' on 19 March 1966. At this time there was less than a year before the elimination of steam traction on the Cambrian. No 75012 remained allocated to Shrewsbury (6D) MPD until withdrawn in January 1967. *T. B. Owen*

Above:
The fireman of double-chimneyed BR Standard Class 4 No 75071 will be preparing to exchange the single-line token with signalman Ossie Davies at Cemmes Road on 7 August 1965. On both sides of the track can be seen the tablet-catching apparatus; the devices carried a lamp fitting for night operation. The station and yard of the former branch to Dinas Mawddwy, which lingered on until 1952, lay to the north of the signalbox on the right. Formerly allocated to depots on the Southern Region of BR, No 75071 was working the 11.05am Aberystwyth-Manchester train. *G. F. Bannister*

Left:
BR Standard Class 4 No 75012 tackles the 1 in 163 grade as it approaches Commins Coch Halt with the up 'Cambrian Coast Express' on 19 March 1966. By this time only the 'CCE', freight, mail and summer Saturday extras were in the hands of steam traction, all other services being operated by diesels, mainly DMUs. *T. B. Owen*

Right:
Some four months earlier on 28 December 1965, BR 'Standard' 4-6-0s Nos 75063 and 75053 present an impressive spectacle as they pound the grade towards Llanbrynmair at Commins Coch. Ill-kempt, care-worn and looking more like refugees from Barry scrapyard, the pair had only months left in traffic before withdrawal from Shrewsbury (6D) MPD. *T. B. Owen*

Above:
This delightful study, taken looking east through Llanbrynmair station on 8 August 1964, shows BR Standard Class 4 No 75024 making a cautious descent of the 1 in 52 grade into the platform with the 8.20am Paddington-Pwllheli train. The station itself was unusual in that it had a split platform on the down side allowing access for road traffic which passed through the middle of the station. This quirk of construction came about after the original short platform was extended, thus leaving the road through the middle. Also clearly visible is the single-line token apparatus with its own lamp for operation during the hours of darkness. *P. W. Gray*

Right:
Looking west towards the station at Llanbrynmair, this view on 20 August 1966 depicts well-groomed 'Standard' 4-6-0 No 75056 piloting an unidentified member of the same class at the head of a Pwllheli-Paddington train. Judging by the volume of black smoke being emitted from the chimneys of both locomotives, the train crews are getting their engines well-prepared for the assault of the 3½ miles of 1 in 52/56 to Talerddig summit. At Llanbrynmair (389ft above sea level) the train had already climbed grades of 1 in 60/78 since leaving Machynlleth (which is 78ft above sea level). *T. B. Owen*

Left:
Another classic study taken east of Llanbrynmair station shows BR Standard Class 4 No 75012 working the up 'Cambrian Coast Express' on 19 March 1966. The stone used for the construction of the road and river bridges was excavated from the cutting at Talerddig.
T. B. Owen

Above:
'Manor' 4-6-0 No 7827 *Lydham Manor* (now preserved on the Torbay Steam Railway) drifts down the 1 in 52 gradient into Llanbrynmair with the down 'Cambrian Coast Express' on 8 August 1964. With the route having passed into the control of the London Midland Region in 1963, the train carries the reporting number

'1M12' denoting that it originated on the Western Region and was passing on to the London Midland.
T. B. Owen

45

Left:
Shrouded in steam in the sub-zero temperature, 'Manor' No 7827 *Lydham Manor* presents an awe-inspiring sight for the photographer as it climbs the 1 in 52 towards Talerddig summit with a passenger train for Shrewsbury on 28 December 1964. *T. B. Owen*

Right:
Crossing Bell's Bridge on the climb to Talerddig, BR 4-6-0 No 75004 pilots 'Manor' No 7822 *Foxcote Manor* with a Barmouth-Birmingham train on 22 August 1964. Originally it was planned to build a tunnel at Talerddig, but this was discounted in favour of a cutting which would provide stone for bridges and other structures. The final 120ft-deep cutting was the deepest in the world at the time of construction. When built, the steep gradients at Talerddig required heavier track, double-headed rail on cast chairs being used, while other parts of the system in 1860 were more commonly laid with flat-bottom rail. *T. B. Owen*

Also crossing Bell's Bridge, BR Standard Class 4 No 75047 makes a steady climb to Talerddig with a freight originating from the coast line. One of the most familiar photographic locations on the GWR, Bell's Bridge, as it was known to legions of Cambrian men, was thought to be named after a mason involved in its construction. In the consist near the rear of the train are two gunpowder vans, presumably from Cookes Explosives at Penrhyndeudraeth. The climb to Talerddig summit was one of the most popular spots for railway photographers as trains, often double-headed, pounded their way to the summit. Whilst steam specials have now been introduced over this route, many of the classic locations have become overgrown. *M. Mensing*

Less than one mile from Talerddig summit, at milepost 62, BR 'Standard' 4-6-0 No 75012 pilots an unidentified member of the same class with a Pwllheli-Birmingham train on 20 August 1966. Whilst BR steam over Talerddig finished on 4 March 1967, with the grime-encrusted BR Standard Class 4 No 75021 hauling the last down 'Cambrian Coast Express', it was to be preserved sister locomotive No 75069 which was to haul the first steam-hauled train over the line in 20 years when British Rail reintroduced such services. On 16 June 1987, with just the barest trace of a slip at Llanbrynmair, and sanders on from around mid-distance, the steam-tight No 75069 and its seven coach, 285-ton load, flew over the top at 32 mph. *T. B. Owen*

Left:

Less than steam-tight BR Standard Class 4s, Nos 75053 and 75063 are seen blasting up the final section of the 1 in 52 gradient, under superb lighting conditions, with the up 'Cambrian Coast Express' on 28 December 1965. Winter conditions at this exposed location were not always so calm, the very vulnerable Talerddig often suffering the ravages of severe weather with raging storms which on occasions led to serious landslips. Fortunately, on these occasions, passengers have only been inconvenienced by having to be transferred, with their luggage, to road transport for a few miles while the line was being cleared. *T. B. Owen*

Below:

The exposed location of the station at Talerddig, at 693ft above sea level, is clearly evident in this picture taken on 8 August 1964. The down waiting-room appears to have suffered from subsidence and exposure to a severe gale. A stop at Talerddig station for up trains was often to allow a pilot locomotive or banker to be detached from the train. *P. W. Gray*

Left:
With the distant for Carno just out of view, BR Standard Class 4s Nos 75053 and 75063 still have steam on as they head down the 1 in 128 grade towards Pontdolgoch with the up 'Cambrian Coast Express' on 28 December 1965. *T. B. Owen*

Right:
Three miles east of Carno, near Clatter, 'Standard' 4-6-0 No 75002 tackles the 1 in 132 grade with a Paddington-Pwllheli train on 22 August 1964. Whilst not as steep as the eastbound climb to Talerddig, the westbound ascent between Moat Lane Junction and Talerddig summit includes some stretches of 1 in 71 and 1 in 100. No 75002 was to survive on Cambrian metals until December 1966 when it was reallocated from Machynlleth (6F) MPD to Croes Newydd (6C) MPD, where it worked until transfer to Stoke (5D) MPD in June 1967, withdrawal coming only two months later. *T. B. Owen*

Left:
Photographers desperately vie to record the passing of the last down 'Cambrian Coast Express' as it stops at Newtown on 4 March 1967. Bearing the correct reporting number, a headboard stating 'Last Cambrian Coast Express – 1967' and a wreath, the passage of BR Standard Class 4 No 75021 not only marked the end of BR steam on the Cambrian, but also the end of through train working from Paddington beyond Birmingham.

After arrival at Aberystwyth, No 75021 was serviced and returned to Shrewsbury with the last steam-hauled mail. While several of her Shrewsbury-allocated sisters went for scrap, No 75021 was transferred to Carnforth (10A) MPD where she survived until February 1968. Ironically, after two months in store at Carnforth, No 75021 was towed to Scotland, where she was broken up at Ward's scrapyard at Inverkeithing. *T. B. Owen*

Above:
Better days over two years earlier see an unidentified 'Manor' 4-6-0 heading an up passenger working from Aberystwyth near Forden on 27 November 1964. Traversing the double-track section between Buttington Junction and Forden, the train is about to cross the River Severn at Cilcewyth Weir. *T. B. Owen*

On 14 November 1964 'Manor' No 7803 *Barcote Manor* has arrived at Welshpool with the up 'Cambrian Coast Express'. BR Standard Class 4 No 75026 waits alongside with a connecting service to Oswestry. Two months later, on 18 January 1965, the line from Whitchurch to Buttington Junction, then part of the London Midland Region, fell under the Beeching 'axe' – 104 years after it was opened. *T. B. Owen*

'Dukedog' No 9027 is pictured arriving at Welshpool with a military special in July 1953. With the locomotives downgraded to power Class 'A' at the end of 1955, work for the remaining 'Dukedogs' was diminishing, although two newly-formed preserved nar- row-gauge lines – the Talyllyn and Festiniog railways – brought their members to the Cambrian lines for their AGMs. Initially, the 'Dukedogs' found work on these specials, although later some strange visitors were to find their way to Cambrian metals. In 1955 an ex-LSWR 'T9' 4-4-0 piloted No 9027 and in 1956 an ex-SECR 'D' class 4-4-0 piloted 'Dean Goods' 0-6-0 No 2538 and, finally, in 1957 ex-L&Y 2-4-2T No 50781 piloted No 9021. *J. M. Jarvis*

Above:
Still carrying evidence of its GWR ownership, 'Duke-dog' No 9024 has yet to receive its BR cast-iron front numberplate, its number being carried in true GWR fashion on the front buffer beam. Later withdrawn from Craven Arms sub-shed in August 1957, No 9024 was photographed at Welshpool on 4 July 1953. By January 1958, only eight members of the class survived, of which only five lasted into the final year of service,

1960. The last two survivors, Nos 9014 and 9017 were based at Croes Newydd and Machynlleth. *J. M. Jarvis*

Right:
Ex-GWR 'Dean Goods' 0-6-0 No 2538 poses for the camera at Welshpool in April 1956. This locomotive was working the 9.15am, Tuesdays, Thursdays and Saturdays only, Oswestry-Newtown Class K freight diagram which included a trip up the Kerry branch

(which ran from Abermule to Kerry). These workings were generally handled by the last of the 'Dean Goods' 0-6-0s and, accordingly, attracted visits by numerous enthusiasts who were anxious to see them struggle with the steep grades. The last two survivors of this class, Nos 2516 and 2538, were retained for this working until the Kerry branch closed on 1 May 1956. *T. B. Owen*

BR Standard Class 4 No 75012 makes good progress as she climbs up the final section of 1 in 53 grade to Breidden with the up 'Cambrian Coast Express' on 19 March 1966. Whilst not strictly on former Cambrian Railways metals, the section between Buttington Junction and Shrewsbury was formerly under GWR/LNWR control and played an important part in the operation of trains originating or terminating on the Cambrian. Having operated as a through service from Paddington since 1921, it wasn't until 1922 that the inaugural run of 'The Cambrian Coast Express' departed from Paddington at 10.20am for Aberystwyth and Pwllheli. After the disruption of World War 2, it was 1951 before British Railways reinstated the train as a daily working. After stopping at Banbury and Birmingham Snow Hill, the train would work non-stop from Wolverhampton to Welshpool via the Abbey Foregate curve at Shrewsbury but, in the 1960s, a stop at Shrewsbury was added where the train reversed. With the 'Cambrian Coast Express' Aberystwyth was reached in just under six hours from Paddington. *T. B. Owen*

Taken from the same vantage point as the previous picture, No 75012 has steam to spare as it heads towards the then-closed station at Breidden. Formerly named Middletown, the station's goods yard was on the left of the train behind the locomotive. This panoramic view gives a good impression of the rolling countryside to be found in this part of the Shropshire-Montgomeryshire borderlands. *T. B. Owen*

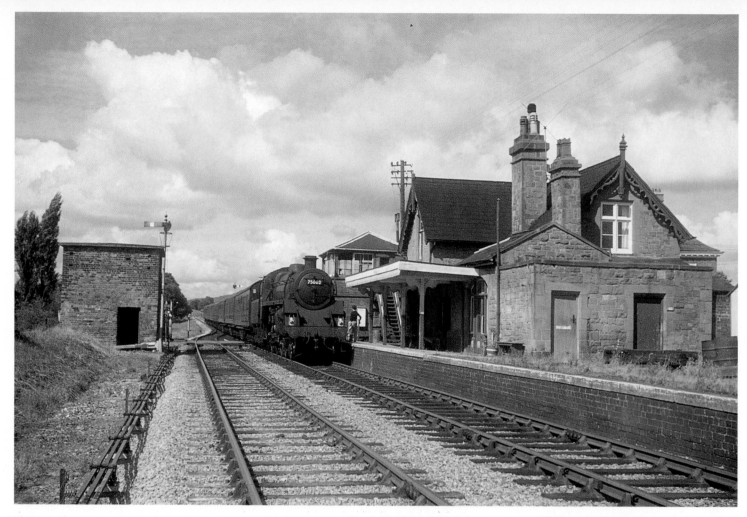

Above:
BR Standard Class 4 No 75004 brings the 7.30am Pwllheli-Paddington service through the closed Westbury (Salop) station on an August Saturday in 1964. The station lay 11 miles west of Shrewsbury and one mile north of the village. The Shrewsbury & Welshpool Railway Co, incorporated in 1856 with powers to build a line 17 miles long between Shrewsbury and Buttington Junction (then Cefn), did not open until 27 January 1862 and, from the first, was used and maintained by the LNWR. The line formed a direct link to the Cambrian Railways main line from the West Midlands. This strategic route was acquired by the LNWR/GWR in 1865; however, intermediate traffic was never very heavy and all stations on the S&W closed to passenger traffic on 12 September 1960. Today, Westbury survives as the only crossing loop on the single line between Sutton Bridge Junction, Shrewsbury, and Welshpool. It retains its station building (now converted as a private dwelling) on the up side and signalbox. The box was a fine example of one of the early 'Joint Line' all-brick cabins with a Saxby & Farmer design influence. Built in the 1870s, it survived until 1991. *G. F. Bannister*

Right:
'Manor' No 7820 *Dinmore Manor* heads a passenger working from Welshpool to Shrewsbury near Hanwood in September 1964. The trackbed shows recent lifting of the double track section between Shrewsbury and Cruckmeole Junction, where the branch to Minsterley joined the main line. *D. Penney*

After reversal at Shrewsbury, the down 'Cambrian Coast Express' leaves Platform No 4 for the Cambrian section on 21 August 1962 behind 'Manor' No 7802 *Bradley Manor*. 12 September 1960 saw the closure of intermediate stations on the Welshpool line, although there were still six passenger trains in each direction in addition to the 'CCE'. With the retiming of the 'CCE' in early 1960, it enabled a return through working between Aberystwyth and Shrewsbury, a task normally entrusted to Machynlleth's best 'Manor' 4-6-0. The locomotive had only a 51min turn round time at Shrewsbury. *P. W. Gray*

Not strictly on a former Cambrian Railways route, this fine portrait of 'Dukedog' No 9017 was taken at Ruabon whilst working a Festiniog Railway Society special in March 1958. Together with No 9014, No 9017 was one of the of last two members of the class in traffic. They were withdrawn in October 1960. Following a period in store at Oswestry Works until February 1962, No 9017 entered preservation and worked under its own steam to Old Oak Common (81A) MPD on 14 February. It was then despatched to the Bluebell Railway where it became the first, and only, GWR loco to be taken into Bluebell stock. *P. J. Hughes*

Left:
Photographed at Brecon, Ivatt 'Mogul' No 46513 stands in the station on 20 August 1962 whilst another member of the same class departs with the 6.00pm to Three Cocks Junction and Hereford. Whilst Brecon did not formally belong to the Cambrian Railways, the company had running powers over the section from Talyllyn Junction. *P. W. Gray*

Above:
Talyllyn Junction station sees activity on 21 August 1962 as Ivatt Class 2 No 46513 stands with the 10.25am Brecon-Hereford train and ex-GWR 0-6-0PT No 3747 arrives with the 8.03am Newport-Brecon service. Talyllyn Junction was the end of the Mid-Wales Railway Co line, although the Cambrian had running powers over the Brecon & Merthyr Railway into Brecon itself. The Hereford, Hay & Brecon Railway (later to become part of the Midland Railway) joined the Mid-Wales at Three Cocks Junction. Thus, neither of the trains in the picture is strictly operating a former Cambrian service. *P. W. Gray*

Three Cocks Junction springs to life as the fireman of Ivatt Class 2 No 46513 prepares to hand over the token from the 10.20am train from Brecon to Hereford on 21 August 1962. From here, this train left former Cambrian Railways metals to traverse the former Midland Railway route to Hereford. Sister locomotive No 46507 waits to take the former Cambrian Railways route to Moat Lane Junction with the 11.15am to Builth Road. *P. W. Gray*

This cameo study depicts Ivatt Mogul No 46510 working the Blodwell Junction-Nantmawr Quarry branch in April 1965. The train is leaving White Gates crossing north of Llanddu with empty limestone wagons from Oswestry. This short branch of one mile 34 chains had a ruling gradient of 1 in 42. Opened in 1866 it became the northwest extremity of the ill-fated Potteries, Shrewsbury & North Wales Railway. Whilst the 'Potts' main line closed in 1880, stone traffic on the Nantmawr section continued consecutively under the Cambrian, the GWR and British Railways. *G. F. Bannister*

Left:
This August 1963 picture shows Ivatt Class 2 No 46512 at Oswestry with a train for the Llanfyllin branch. The first railway to reach the market town of Oswestry was opened on 23 December 1848 in the form of a 2½-mile branch from Gobowen. For 13 years this branch provided the only rail link between Oswestry and the rest of the country, until the Oswestry & Newtown opened for traffic in 1861. Upon the formation of the Cambrian Railways on 27 July 1864, Oswestry became the headquarters of the company and was where the railway's main offices and locomotive works were situated. The 8 mile 41 chains branch from Llanymynech to Llanfyllin closed on 18 January 1965 – 102 years after it had opened. *D. Penney*

Above:
Ivatt 'Mogul' No 46514 arrives at Frankton Halt with an early morning Whitchurch to Oswestry train on 27 November 1964. *R. Hobbs*

Above:
The 5.03pm Wrexham Central-Ellesmere auto-train leaves Hightown Halt, Wrexham, on Easter Monday, 1960, with 0-4-2T No 1438 in charge. Hightown Halt, 12 miles from Ellesmere, was the last stop on the line and was opened in July 1923. The station consisted merely of a nameboard and a noticeboard on a short platform without any form of shelter for intending pas-

sengers. From here the line climbed swiftly at 1 in 65 on an embankment high above industrial buildings before running close to the foot of Wrexham's famous 15th century church tower. Following the last day of passenger services on 8 September 1962, the line was truncated to Marchwiel. Freight traffic served the remaining section until final closure on 27 March 1965. *M. Mensing*

Right:
Ivatt Class 2 No 46520 shunts empty coaching stock at Dolgelly on 28 November 1964. The Cambrian formed an end-on junction with the GWR at Dolgelly, the former having arrived from Barmouth by way of the Aberystwyth & Welsh Coast Railway. The GWR station buildings were situated on the up side of the station and the Cambrian on the down. *R. Hobbs*

Below:
Vale of Rheidol locomotive No 9 *Prince of Wales* is returned to narrow gauge metals on 20 April 1960, following overhaul at Swindon Works. *T. B. Owen*

Right:
No 9 *Prince of Wales* leaves Aberystwyth for Devil's Bridge in August 1963. The train is traversing the section from the old terminus. Services were diverted to operate from the main line station from 20 May 1968. No 9 was repainted in its original Cambrian Railways livery of yellow ochre in 1982 to mark not only the line's 80th anniversary, but also the locomotive's own 80th birthday. The engine was formally recommissioned at a ceremony on Easter Sunday, 10 April 1982. *D. Penney*

Left:
Still carrying its full GWR livery, Vale of Rheidol No 7, then unnamed, leaves Aberffrwd with a train for Devil's Bridge on 1 September 1953. Upon Nationalisation in 1948, two sister locomotives Nos 8 and 9 received the new owner's livery, whilst No 7 proclaimed its GWR ownership until 1954. In 1956 the Western Region, probably inspired by the success of the nearby Talyllyn and realising that they possessed a potential tourist attraction, painted the three loco-

motives in Brunswick Green and the coaching stock in GWR brown and cream. At the same time the locomotives were given names: No 7 became *Owain Glyndŵr*, No 8 *Llywelyn* and No 9 regained the name *Prince of Wales* which it had carried under Vale of Rheidol and Cambrian ownership. *T. B. Owen*

Above:
Carrying the unlined BR livery No 7, is seen ¾-mile after leaving Rheidol Falls Halt on 3 August 1955. The

falls can be seen on the bottom right hand side of the picture and the local landmark known as 'The Stag' – a result of earlier leadworkings, can be seen on the far side of the valley. Whilst BR had divested itself of many lines, both standard and narrow gauge, during the 1950s, it retained the Vale of Rheidol route as a steam-operated line well after main line steam ceased elsewhere on the network in 1968. It was only to be sold to preservationists in the mid-1980s – an event which marked the demise of regular BR steam. *T. B. Owen*

77

A delightful study of a long forgotten age: Welshpool & Llanfair Railway 0-6-0T No 822 prepares to leave Llanfair Caereinion with a goods train for Welshpool on 17 May 1956. During the 1950s services on the line were limited to one daily goods train leaving Welshpool before midday. Passenger services on the line had ceased in February 1931, but the last goods train working ran until only six months after this picture was taken on 5 November 1956. Happily, thanks to the magnificent efforts of the Welshpool & Llanfair Light Railway Preservation Co, the pleasure of narrow gauge rail travel can once again be enjoyed.

T. B. Owen

Finding a narrow slot between the houses and parked cars, Welshpool & Llanfair No 822 works bunker first with an up freight across Church Street, Welshpool, in September 1956. Had an 1845 Brunel broad-gauge proposal come to fruition the railway would have used a deep tunnel under Welshpool and a 92ft viaduct across the River Banwy. Nothing came of this, or of several later narrow-gauge proposals, until the passing of the Light Railways Act of 1896 which gave fresh heart to the promoters. The 2ft 6in gauge line opened on 4 April 1903. *T. J. Edginton/Colour-Rail*

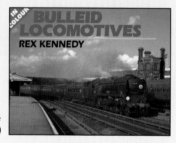